the GRIZZLIES

of GROUSE MOUNTAIN

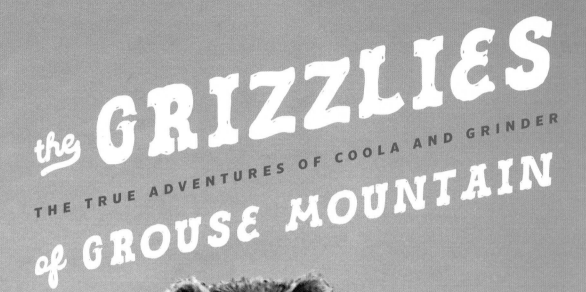

the GRIZZLIES

THE TRUE ADVENTURES OF COOLA AND GRINDER

of GROUSE MOUNTAIN

Shelley Hrdlitschka and **Rae Schidlo**

illustrated by **Linda Sharp**

VICTORIA
VANCOUVER
CALGARY

Heritage House Publishing Ltd.
heritagehouse.ca

Cataloguing information available from Library and Archives Canada

978-1-77203-277-2 (cloth)

Edited by Lara Kordic
Cover and interior design by Jacqui Thomas
Photographs on pages 36–37 by Devin Manky and Sylvia Dolson,
courtesy of Grouse Mountain Refuge for Endangered Wildlife

The interior of this book was produced on FSC®-certified, acid-free paper,
processed chlorine free, and printed with vegetable-based inks.

We acknowledge the financial support of the Government of Canada through
the Canada Book Fund (CBF) and the Canada Council for the Arts, and the
Province of British Columbia through the British Columbia Arts Council
and the Book Publishing Tax Credit.

23 22 21 20 19 1 2 3 4 5

Printed in China

To WILDLIFE CONSERVATIONISTS EVERYWHERE

Distances

BELLA COOLA TO INVERMERE—*1,209 kilometres*

VANCOUVER TO BELLA COOLA—*993 kilometres*

VANCOUVER TO INVERMERE—*857 kilometres*

Grouse Mountain Facts

PEAK OF GROUSE MOUNTAIN ELEVATION—*1,200 metres*

GRIZZLY HABITAT ELEVATION—*1,100 metres*

LENGTH OF GROUSE GRIND HIKING TRAIL—*2.9 kilometres*

AVERAGE YEARLY SNOWFALL—*8.7 metres*

NUMBER OF PEOPLE WHO WORK AT THE REFUGE
FOR ENDANGERED WILDLIFE

· *2 permanent staff members*

· *3 to 4 rangers (employed from May to November)*

· *25 to 35 active volunteers at any given time*

PACIFIC
OCEAN

BRITISH COLUMBIA
ALBERTA
HAIDA
GWAII
BELLA COOLA
GROUSE
MOUNTAIN
VANCOUVER
ISLAND
Salish
Sea
VANCOUVER
INVERMERE
USA

TINY GRIZZLY BEAR CUB stumbled out of the forest and lurched across the logging road. Two forestry workers in a red truck watched as the cub struggled to get through the tall grass by the side of the road, falling over sideways again and again. The men waited for a long time, hoping for a mother bear to appear, but she never did. Finally they approached the small bear. They thought he would run away, but he was too weak. He hadn't had any food or water in a long time.

The men knew they had to help. They threw a coat over the cub and placed him in a knapsack in the back of their truck. They took him to a veterinarian in Invermere, a small town tucked up beside the Rocky Mountains in British Columbia.

This little bear—who was later named Grinder, after the famous Grouse Grind hiking trail—weighed only 4.5 kilograms. The vet thought that he had been on his own for at least five days. He injected fluid under the bear's skin to help him get back the water he had lost. The tiny bear was not yet weaned, so the vet fed him only milk. The cub gained 2.5 kilograms in one week, but he was still far too young to survive on his own in the wild.

Around the same time, over one thousand kilometres northwest of Invermere, near Bella Coola, BC, a tiny four-month-old grizzly bear cub padded through the forest behind his mother and two siblings.

Then, a terrible thing happened. The mother crossed a highway and was struck by a truck and killed. Because the cubs had lagged behind, they were not hit. They climbed a tree to get to safety.

Soon conservation officers arrived, but they couldn't reach the cubs, who were too high up in the tree. The only way to rescue the cubs, they believed, was to cut the tree down. Sadly, their plan did not work out as they had hoped. One cub was crushed by the falling tree. Another ran off into the woods, never to be seen again.

The third cub, who was later named Coola, was lucky. The conservation officers rescued him and took him to Bella Coola. Like Grinder, he was not weaned yet, so they gave him milk to drink.

One thousand kilometres south of Bella Coola, near Vancouver, another vet heard about these two orphaned grizzly bear cubs. He knew they were too young to be released into the wild with no mothers to look after them. Usually grizzly bear cubs spend the first two to four years of their lives with their mother. In that time, she teaches them everything they will need to survive on their own.

The vet was also worried about what would happen to the cubs if they were raised in an environment that was not natural for grizzly bears, somewhere they wouldn't be free to wander and forage for food as wild bears do. Then he got an idea.

He called the owners of Grouse Mountain Resort, and together they made a plan. They would build a five-acre wildlife refuge on the mountain where the cubs could live and thrive. Thanks to the vet's quick thinking and the Grouse Mountain Resort owners' willingness to build the refuge, the lives of the two little bears were spared.

While the refuge was being built, Grinder and Coola travelled to a farm close to Grouse Mountain. They stayed in a barn and developed a strong bond, spending a lot of time wrestling, much as puppies do.

Even at such a young age, the bears had very different personalities. Grinder would try to coax Coola to play, when all Coola wanted to do was sleep. Grinder would poke at him and nibble his ear. Eventually Coola would give Grinder a shove with his paw. As long as Grinder got a reaction from Coola, he was happy. They behaved like brothers.

There were physical differences between them, too. Grinder was slightly smaller and a lighter colour. Coola was heavier and darker.

With no mother bear around to teach them and watch out for them, Coola and Grinder had to learn most things the hard way, through trial and error. Fortunately, they had human caregivers to provide food and keep them safe.

*T*he day finally came for the cubs to move to their new permanent home on Grouse Mountain. Their human caregivers lured them into crates and drove them to the base of the mountain. Then they all loaded onto the Skyride and rode to the top of the mountain. When they got to the bears' habitat, the doors to their crates were opened for their release.

Coola scampered out of his crate first and began checking out his new home. Grinder emerged from his crate a bit more cautiously. Soon he joined Coola in exploring the refuge, which had forests, berry bushes, ponds for swimming, grasses to roam through, logs to scratch, and rocks to lie on in the sunshine. They also discovered the fence that went around the whole habitat. They found out quickly that the fence would give them a slight shock if they touched it, so they learned to avoid it.

The bears were hungry and began to eat the grasses, roots, berries, and grubs that they found on their own. To make sure they were keeping up their strength, the wildlife rangers scattered sweet potatoes, carrots, and apples throughout the habitat so the bears would learn to forage and exercise. Later the rangers introduced meat and a dog kibble with added vitamins and minerals. The bears thrived.

MAP LEGEND

1. Eye of the Wind windmill
2. The Lions (mountains)
3. Grouse Mountain
4. Lower Pond
5. Upper Pond
6. Baby Bear Den
7. Ski Wee building (where bear food is stored)
8. Yurt
9. Bear Den (where the bears hibernate)
🎥 Bear Cam

GRIZZLY BEAR
HABITAT

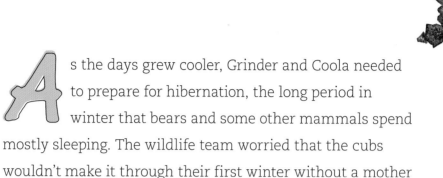

As the days grew cooler, Grinder and Coola needed to prepare for hibernation, the long period in winter that bears and some other mammals spend mostly sleeping. The wildlife team worried that the cubs wouldn't make it through their first winter without a mother bear to show them what to do.

In the fall all grizzly bears enter a phase called hyperphagia, which means they are hungry all the time. They need to gain a lot of weight in order to live off their own fat through the winter. When Grinder and Coola arrived at Grouse Mountain, they weighed less than ten kilograms each, but by November of that first year, Grinder weighed sixty kilograms and Coola was seventy-five kilograms.

In the wild, bears prepare dens to hibernate in. To help the cubs out, the wildlife team built a small log house that the bears could use as a den. They placed boughs from fir trees in the den for bedding, and attached a video camera to a wall so that the rangers could watch the bears during the winter.

As winter approached, the young bears began to spend more time in the man-made den. They got tired and began eating the bark off trees. This bark creates a plug, like a cork, which lodges at the bottom of their intestine, preventing them from getting rid of any waste during hibernation. When the bears settled down and fell asleep for the winter, the rangers closed and locked the door to the den. Like all hibernating bears, they stopped eating and drinking for the next few months.

The fences around the refuge were taken down, and the mountain top became a ski resort again. Most of the skiers, snowboarders, and snowshoers didn't know that two small bears were sleeping in the little log house.

During that first winter, the rangers kept a close eye on the video that was being streamed from inside the snug den. They saw that the bears actually got up and moved about the den each day, stretching their muscles and tidying up their beds. Grizzly bears are not true hibernators like some other mammals. Instead, they go into a state of dormancy. This means their heart and breathing slow down, and their body temperature drops slightly, but they still wake up for a while each day. If they did not move during dormancy, their muscles would get so weak that they would not be able to stand.

BEAR DEN

AVERAGE SNOW DEPTH—12 METRES

Four months passed. The little bears continued to sleep with their daily wakeful periods, which were all caught on camera. When the snow began to melt and the days grew longer, the rangers noticed that the bears were staying awake for longer periods each day. They replaced the fencing around the habitat and opened the door to their den.

Grinder appeared first, followed by Coola.

The little bears had survived the winter on their own!

And they were hungry! The first thing bears often look for in spring is skunk cabbage, a long green broad-leafed plant with a yellow-stemmed flower in the centre. Because the refuge had no skunk cabbage, the rangers hid heads of Romaine lettuce in the bears' habitat. Grinder and Coola sniffed out the lettuce and headed straight for the snow banks to dig their way to a feast. The roughage allowed the plug in their intestine to pass through the body. Once they had their fill, they played in the snow, sliding down the banks and rolling on their backs.

As the snow melted, the bears started foraging again. The rangers slowly added vegetables, fruits, and protein kibble. They introduced root vegetables first, followed by fruits. Coola and Grinder *loved* treats like honey and grapes. Later in the summer, they got whole watermelons, which they bobbed for in the ponds.

Gradually they also got more protein. Salmon is their favourite. Every September through November, they receive extra protein every day to help them gain the weight they need for their dormancy period.

Each fall, when the bears refuse to come out, even for treats, the rangers know it's time to close the den door.

By the time they went into their second dormancy, Grinder weighed 151 kilograms and Coola was 189 kilograms.

Coastal bears, like Coola, tend to be bigger than interior bears, like Grinder, because their diet includes more protein, mainly in the form of salmon. This is why Coola has always had a larger body size than Grinder. Today, as full-grown bears, Coola weighs about 450 kilograms, and Grinder weights 400 kilograms before their dormancy period.

It's unusual for two male grizzlies to live together like Coola and Grinder do. Because there is enough food, and there are no females to fight over, they have never had any reason to be aggressive towards one another.

They enjoy each other's company. Even when they sleep, they are usually side by side.

Sometimes they play-fight with their huge mouths open, trying to grab the other's thick fur around the neck. Sometimes Grinder is like a pesky younger brother and invades Coola's space, even when Coola is napping. If Grinder finishes his food first, he'll walk over to where Coola is eating and watch him, trying to make Coola feel uncomfortable about not sharing.

Coola is cool. He lets Grinder look on as if he doesn't care. If Grinder gets too nosey, Coola will swat him and give a soft growl. Grinder backs off for a few seconds and then returns to annoy Coola some more.

During the day, Coola and Grinder behave as they would in the wild. Most of their waking time is spent foraging for food. Anything and everything is game, even a bird that is too slow nibbling on a berry. Then the bears sleep, allowing the food to digest.

When they wake up again they may swim, doing all kinds of poses in the water. They love to float on their backs, grabbing their hind feet with their front paws. They dig around in the bottom of the ponds for sticks or stones, which they then toss into the air. They may even find it interesting to watch us as we watch them!

Once in a while, Coola and Grinder need the vet to do a full medical check-up in their den. The vet checks their weight, blood, teeth, and overall health. They have to be tranquilized with a dart, one bear at a time. This makes them sleep so the vet can safely examine them.

One time, Coola went first. The tranquilizing dart didn't make it through his thick fur and skin, and he started shuffling around, turning over rocks in the den, and snorting. Grinder, who was locked out of the den, sensed all this. He paced back and forth past the closed door and tried to look in through the wired windows. He then sat down but could not relax. He began pacing again.

The bears' bond is so deep that Grinder knew Coola was in trouble, even though they were apart.

Finally, with a second dart, Coola fell asleep, and Grinder lumbered off into the forest.

Another time, the wildlife staff noticed that Coola was more sluggish than usual. The vet checked his scat and decided that he needed medicine. He would have to take ten to twelve pills twice a day. The wildlife team stuffed each pill into a marshmallow and Coola just waited patiently as each marshmallow was thrown within his reach.

Grinder and Coola are unique. Because they were orphaned as cubs and hand-fed by humans while they were little, they have an unusual relationship with people. For this reason they cannot be released into the wild. If they did, they might become "problem" bears and have to be destroyed. However, their lives on Grouse Mountain give them the room to forage, roam, and play like all bears do.

They have also taught us humans a lot. The rangers who study their behaviour have learned what cubs know by instinct and what they learn from their mother. The rangers now know better ways to manage other orphaned grizzly cubs, raising them in habitats like the one on Grouse Mountain, but with the plan of releasing them into the wild when they are old enough to survive on their own.

Today, Coola and Grinder are ambassadors for their species. Thousands of visitors from all over the world come to see them each year, feel their magnificent presence, and learn the importance of conserving bear species and protecting bears for years to come.

the BEAR

GRINDER

Blond-tipped coat

340 to 400 kilograms adult weight, pre-hibernation

2.2 metres tall, standing

Dark-coloured claws, 13 centimetres in length

Curious personality

Likes to bluff charge

FACTS

COOLA

Dark brown coat

400 to 450 kilograms adult weight, pre-hibernation

2.5 metres tall, standing

Light coloured claws, 13 centimetres in length

Laid-back personality

DID · YOU

- Grizzly bears have a better **sense of smell** than a hound dog and can detect food almost 6 kilometres away. Bear noses contain hundreds of tiny muscles. They can move their noses with finger-like dexterity.

- Grizzly bears are considered **carnivores**—or meat eaters—but they are actually **omnivores**, which means they eat both plants and animals. Eighty percent of their diet is plant-based.

- Grizzly bears are **brown bears**. They were given the name grizzly because of their grizzled appearance when their coats have blond tips.

- The **hump** between their shoulders is a mass of muscle, helping them dig for food.

- Grizzly bears weigh about the same as a **grapefruit** when they are born. There can be one to four cubs in a litter.

- Grizzly bears can **run more than 50 kilometres per hour**. They can't keep up this speed for long, as they would risk burning too many calories.

- Grizzly bears **live about twenty years** in the wild and up to **forty years** in captivity.

- A grizzly **bear bed** in a den can be over 1 metre thick with branches.

KNOW?

> In the wild a male grizzly needs approximately **1,000 acres** to find enough food to keep him alive. He needs less land if there is lots of food, security, and mates available.

> Bears lose about **30 percent** of their pre-hibernation body weight during, and for one month following, dormancy.

> Bears are **intelligent, curious**, and have **excellent memory**, particularly about where they can find sources of food. Grizzly bears can remember other bears they have not seen for ten years or more.

> Adult male grizzlies **hibernate** for several weeks, while females that emerge from dens with cubs can hibernate for as long as seven months.

> A bear's body language can help reveal its mood. In general, **bears show agitation** by swaying their heads, huffing, popping their jaws, blowing, and snorting or clacking their teeth. Lowered head and laid-back ears are also signs of aggression.

> Grizzly bears play an important **role in forest ecosystems** as seed dispersers and nutrient providers. Berry seeds pass through the bear unbroken and are able to germinate. Not only that, but they come with their own pile of fresh manure as fertilizer!

DEVIN MANKY

SYLVIA DOLSON

SYLVIA DOLSON

SYLVIA DOLSON

DEVIN MANKY

ACKNOWLEDGEMENTS

THIS BOOK WOULD not have been possible without the support and input of the amazing team at Grouse Mountain. Special thanks to Dr. Ken Macquisten, Director of the Grouse Mountain Refuge for Endangered Wildlife, and the veterinarian who brought the bears to Grouse Mountain. Thanks also to Devin Manky, Wildlife Manager at Grouse Mountain; Colleen Johnson, Grouse Mountain Education Director; and wildlife rangers Kevin Langford, Kris Georgiev, and Maria Lancaster. Thank you also to Jennifer Cooper, Bill Cooper, Laurie Cooper, and Julie Rudd, whose beautiful photos informed many of the illustrations in this book.

ABOUT THE AUTHORS

SHELLEY HRDLITSCHKA is a long-time resident of North Vancouver, home of Coola and Grinder. She discovered her love for children's literature while teaching school and was inspired her to write her own books. She is now the award-winning author of several novels for teens, including *Lost Boy, Sister Wife* (shortlisted for the Governor General's Literary Award), and *Dancing in the Rain*. When she is not reading or writing, she can be found hiking, snowshoeing, Zumba dancing, or hanging out with the grizzly bears at the Grouse Mountain Refuge for Endangered Wildlife.

Born and raised in Saskatchewan, **RAE SCHIDLO** knew from the age of six that she wanted to be a teacher. She holds a Bachelor of Education degree from the University of Saskatchewan and a Master's of Education from the University of British Columbia, and enjoyed a long career in the field that she loves. Now retired and living in North Vancouver, she spends her time hiking, cycling, swimming, gardening, reading, line dancing, and volunteering at the Grouse Mountain Refuge for Endangered Wildlife.

LINDA SHARP holds a Bachelor of Fine Arts degree from the University of Alberta. She works in fabric and paint, using oilsticks to capture movement and visual energy. Linda volunteers with North Vancouver Community Players and Theatre West Van, designing graphics and painting sets. She lives in North Vancouver.

GROUSE MOUNTAIN REFUGE FOR ENDANGERED WILDLIFE

Grouse Mountain Refuge for Endangered Wildlife is a wilderness sanctuary where endangered animals can explore and play, knowing they're safe and secure. Visitors will find all this and more at the research, education, and conservation centre on the mountain. The Refuge also offers leading-edge interpretative programs that make learning about nature fun and fascinating.

>> grousemountain.com/wildlife-refuge

GRIZZLY BEAR FOUNDATION

Grizzly Bear Foundation is the only Canadian charitable organization dedicated solely to the welfare of grizzly bears (*Ursus arctos*).

It works collaboratively to support the conservation and preservation of grizzly bears through research and public education. It connects people with the latest research and conservation programs to improve human-bear interactions and empower communities to become better stewards of both grizzly bears and their habitats.

Fifty percent of the royalties for this book will be donated to the Foundation.

>> grizzlybearfoundation.com

THE END